FIBER EXPRESSIONS:
The Contemporary Quilt

QUILT NATIONAL

D0514638

West Chester, Pennsylvania 19380

ACKNOWLEDGMENTS

FIBER EXPRESSIONS: The Contemporary Quilt
Quilt National
Hilary Morrow Fletcher, Quilt National '87 Coordinator
Pamela S. Parker, Executive Director, The Dairy Barn Southeastern Ohio Cultural Arts Center, Athens, Ohio
Members of the Quilt National Committee: Fidella Anderson, Gail Berenson, Suzy Chesser, Kit Dailey, Kathy Dane, Marvin Fletcher, Rosemary Mayronne, Ann Moneypenny, Inez Mullins, Joanne Redlich, Phyllis Rovner, Don Taylor
The Dairy Barn Board of Directors
FAIRFIELD PROCESSING CORPORATION, makers of Poly-fil® batting material, Danbury, Connecticut
The Ohio Arts Council
Opportunities for the Arts, Columbus, Ohio
Peter Schiffer, Schiffer Publishing, Ltd., West Chester, Pennsylvania
Ms. Machiko Izawa, Dentsu Incorporated, New York, New York
The Asahi Shimbun, Tokyo, Japan
Mr. Tetsuya Kotani, APT Advertising Company, Ltd., Tokyo, Japan
Nippon Express U.S.A., Inc.
Paul J. Smith, American Craft Museum, New York, New York
Robert and Ardis James, Chappaqua, New York

EDITOR: Nancy Roe
DESIGNER: Chris Brannon
All photography by BRIAN BLAUSER unless otherwise indicated.

COVER: High Tech Tucks V. (detail), Caryl Bryer Fallert, Oswego, Illinois

This book may be purchased from Quilt National or the publisher.
Please include $2.00 for postage and handling.
Try your bookstore first.

FIBER EXPRESSIONS:
The Contemporary Quilt

INTRODUCTION

Quilt National '87, the fifth in a series of biennial exhibits organized by the Dairy Barn Southeastern Ohio Cultural Arts Center, reveals that interest in the quilt as art form is undiminished.

In fact, the 89 works selected from more than 900 pieces submitted by 430 artists indicate that more and more sculptors, painters, printmakers, potters and artists in other media are seizing on quilts as another avenue to explore and delight in.

A majority of those whose works were juried into Quilt National '87 have a background of formal art training. Many are pursuing careers as teachers, lecturers, workshop leaders, curators, art historians. A number have exhibited widely throughout the United States and abroad and won grants and awards.

It is obvious from the artists' comments on their entries that they revel in the tactile and visual possibilities of the quilt as art form. Many trace their interest in fabric and sewing back to childhood—watching mothers, aunts, grandmothers and great-grandmothers make garments and traditional patchwork and appliqué quilts.

An artist who had concentrated on woodblocks spoke of an "Eureka!" moment when it dawned that blending art and quiltmaking was possible. Another wrote "....a painter, I've come back to my painted images; they're just done in fabric now." Another called her work "textile paintings."

Quilt National '87 reveals the contemporary quilt is still overwhelmingly a woman's art form. Nine men submitted entries, and four had works juried into the exhibit, including Patrick Dorman's "Revelation," which the jurors honored with the "Award of Excellence."

Contemporary quilts continue to gain viewers and creators worldwide, and Quilt National '87 drew entries from 10 nations, with artists from Great Britain, West Germany, France and Japan represented in the show itself.

For one artist, her Quilt National piece was her first contemporary quilt; for another, a 400th. Some had lost track of numbers: Therese May answered "lots" and Mary Morgan, "many, many" to the query about total quilt output.

The artists with works in the exhibit come from settings as varied as Chibaken, Japan, and Painted Post, N.Y. What they have in common is a thoughtful, intense view of their art, pleasure in its potential for spurring creativity, and a desire to share their vision and truths with others.

Many wrote of their roots—or their art's roots—in traditional quilting. Holley Junker paid eloquent homage to this tie with the past when she wrote: "I find the tradition of quilting gives me a connection to women from the past and to women alive whom I will never meet. The quilters I do meet are almost unique among artists, they share and they care."

Quilt National '87 is itself a sharing of the vivid, complex, stimulating world of the contemporary quilt and its creators.

Gerhardt Knodel

Penny McMorris

Jan Myers

ABOUT THE JURORS

Gerhardt Knodel is artist-in-residence and director of the Fiber Department at Cranbrook Academy of Art in Bloomfield Hills, Michigan.

A fiber artist who creates woven small-scale pieces and environmental sculptures, Knodel has had work included in invitational and juried exhibitions throughout the United States and overseas in such shows as the International Bienniale of Tapestry in Lausanne, Switzerland.

His commissions include those for the Xerox Corporation, the Ford Motor Company and the Government Services Administration. He has received several grants, including awards from the National Endowment for the Humanities and the Japan Cultural Commission, and has been the subject of a number of films and videos.

He earned a master of arts degree from California State University at Long Beach.

Penny McMorris produced and hosted 26 programs on quilting shown nationally on the Public Broadcasting System's stations and purchased by the British Broadcasting Corporation.

She is the author of *Crazy Quilts,* published by E.P. Dutton, New York; and co-author of *The Art Quilt,* published by the Quilt Digest Press, San Francisco.

McMorris has lectured extensively and has served as curator of the Owens Corning Collection in Toledo, Ohio.

She holds a master's degree in art history from Bowling Green State University in Bowling Green, Ohio.

Jan Myers is an internationally known quilt artist who has had work in numerous individual and group shows, including Quilt National, American Craft Museum exhibits and The Art Quilt collection (curated by Penny McMorris).

She is represented in many corporate collections, and her work is displayed in major hotels in Atlanta, Georgia; St. Louis, Missouri; Knoxville, Tennessee; and Greenville, South Carolina.

She has lectured and taught throughout the United States and was a workshop leader and lecturer at Quilt National '85.

She holds a master's degree from the University of Minnesota.

JURORS' COMMENTS

The *Quilt National '87* jurors found the jurying process "intense," "exciting," "a challenge," "a learning task."

The three—fiber artists Gerhardt Knodel and Jan Myers and art historian Penny McMorris—viewed and reviewed 915 slides of work by 430 artists. The process was grueling, demanding complete concentration as slide after slide flashed on the screens and the jurors viewed, assessed, commented, discussed, reviewed—and selected slides for each succeeding round of judging.

Once the initial jurying process was completed, the works were sent to the Dairy Barn to be photographed for the catalog. At this stage, one juror returned to Athens to view the quilts themselves and make a final culling of any that—close-up—did not live up to their slide images.

"In the best of all possible worlds, we would be viewing quilts, not slides, there would be no time constraints, and I could respond without my own personal biases and history as a quiltmaker. The first two are impractical; the third, impossible," Jan Myers wrote in her commentary.

The jurors spoke of their respect and regard for the "human effort and aspirations represented by each work," as Myers put it. All regretted the necessity of jurying out 90 percent of the quilts submitted.

Penny McMorris noted her pleasure in the "rare opportunity to see the work of 430 serious quiltmakers from around the world," and her wish that the logistics of such a major international exhibition did not make jurying-by-slide inevitable.

The three jurors agreed in seeing in the 1987 entries trends evident in the previous *Quilt National* exhibits:

"My guess is that if the [*Quilt National '87*] quilts were categorized, we would find that many of them are directly inspired either by a traditional style or by the work of one of a small number of widely publicized innovators in contemporary quiltmaking....," Gerhardt Knodel commented, adding a call for more and more quilt artists to extend their vision outside the field itself when seeking inspiration.

McMorris noted that "many of the quilts shared a common language—floating triangles, worm-shapes, lightning bolts, checks and dots—and common colors—hot pinks, oranges, neon-yellows and black..." which she credited to the influence of the Italian design group Memphis.

More entries had "two designed sides...there was more machine quilting and some more interesting cases of drawing with machine-made stitching lines...and more fine embellishment," she said.

In Myers' view, the entries revealed that "a certain plateau has been reached: there was an overall facility with basic principles of color and design in the great majority of work submitted."

For her, the fact that "many fine quilts are not in *Quilt National '87*...was the most difficult part," explaining that the jurors set aside "several well-designed, well-colored and well-executed pieces...in favor of...less formulaic works."

Underlining a thought expressed by Knodel, Myers commented that the jury "did not view many radical departures from the fabric/batt/fabric format that also contained a solid integrity of image-making." Exceptions she pointed to include Virginia Jacobs' "Krakow Kabuki Waltz," Susan Shie's "Neighborhood with Comet Scar," and Damaris Jackson's "Lines from the Park."

"These pieces represent a certain layering of elements that elevates them: beyond their initial impact, they hold my interest. The whole is greater than the sum of its parts," Myers said.

Knodel expanded on the theme of art as "extending beyond the object with broader implications," stating his view that the "most wonderful Art...provokes questions, stimulates curiosity and establishes relationships to specific conditions of life in a particular time.

"This current moment in the evolving history of quilt-making will be remembered for its competency, its control, for learning the lessons of its own history and passing them on as a legacy to the future," he wrote.

Myers provided insight into the jurying process itself, describing the moment when the shape of the exhibit began to evidence itself:

"While there was no conscious stated effort on the part of the jury to present a 'broad' view either in imagery or technique, I became aware of a certain dynamic as choices were made....the dynamic was...supplied by the pieces themselves...

"At some point, the show began to take on its own life, and further additions were made, in part, relative to those works already included."

In her assessment of the overall result of the jurors' labors, McMorris wrote that "taken as a whole, I find the show the strongest *Quilt National* to date. Perhaps two dozen of its quilts represent the best original quilt design work being done today. The rest serve as a fine example of current trends."

She voiced her hope that the jurors had arrived at a show "that has something for every viewer, that may spark controversy and provide surprise as well as exemplify elegant craftsmanship and design..."

Myers also expressed her hope that the exhibit would challenge viewers: "There are beautiful pieces here, there are powerful pieces, there are pieces you 'wish I had made,' there are pieces you don't believe are in the show."

After taking time to reflect on the jurying process and its resulting exhibit, Myers concluded, "I now feel that all of these pieces make a successful show, one that contributes to the viewers' broadening concept of 'Quilt.'"

Entry Requirements

The Quilt National entry form states that "all work must be an original design of the entrant, not a copy of a traditional design or a variation on an original design of another artist. Original interpretations of traditional design elements are acceptable. The work must be fiber (although not exclusively) and two or more of the following terms must be applicable: pieced, layered, stitched, stuffed."

The resulting Quilt National Exhibit is composed of works which are quilts by virtue of their structure rather than their function. The pieces exist because their creators wanted to make artistic statements using the medium of layered fabric.

COMMENTS FROM
QUILT NATIONAL'S COORDINATOR

I doubt that the job title "coordinator" calls to mind a specific list of duties. Having served in this administrative capacity for three of the five Quilt Nationals, the responsibilities have become almost second nature to me. Coordinating an event like *Quilt National* is a job which is characterized by long-range planning, attention o detail and varying levels of intensity. There are times over the two-year course of the job when it becomes the number one priority in my life as well as the life of my very supportive family. As with any job there are elements which I would like to change but over which I have no control. Why, then, do I elect to do this job again and again? The answer is really quite simple—*Quilt National* is a labor of love!

I love being intimately involved with the process of watching a *Quilt National* develop from a mountain of entries—most of which arrive within three or four days—to the maze of color, shape and texture which the visitor sees. There is the excitement of processing each entry, studying the slides and being amazed by the level of creative energy that they represent. There is the respect that goes with observing the jurors' deliberations as they discuss the strengths and weaknesses of what they see. With the arrival of each parcel addressed to *Quilt National* there is the anticipation and joy of discovering the treasure inside. The quilts very quickly become "mine." As I stroll through the exhibition before anyone else arrives, each one shares a message or gives me something new to see. And, of course, there is the sorrow that comes with the realization that as I return the works to their respective boxes, I must say "good-bye."

Above all, however, is the fact that I love the people. *Quilt National* has provided me an opportunity to learn so much—from the jurors, the artists, the photographer, the designers and the visitors. The jurors, photographer and designers have taught me new ways to "see" not only quilts, but my whole world. Meeting the artists gives me insights into the creative process and how their lives are influenced by what they do. Lastly, there are the visitors: those who already love quilts the way that I do and those who don't. Listening to the visitors' comments is like experiencing the quilts for the first time through their eyes. There is endless joy in sharing what I love with others.

Coordinating *Quilt National* can be tedious, boring and, at times, hard work. These moments are relatively few and are far outnumbered by the times of exhilaration, satisfaction and pure pleasure. As the exhibit's coordinator, I am indeed a very fortunate person.

Hilary Fletcher
Quilt National '87
Coordinator

Patrick Dorman
Seattle, Washington
Revelation
Cotton fabric, cotton batting, mother-of-pearl buttons, glass buttons and beads. Hand quilted, hand appliquéd, spot stitch beading, beaded net. 83″ x 92″

"Revelation" is the celebration of the sacred mystery of life. The mandala of Earth, Air, Water and Fire is surrounded by the images which mark the passage of time: rising and setting sun, seasons of the year, cycles of the moon. My representational shadow floats within this place and time. The buttons and net are the mystery and spirit which bind the cosmos.

Award of Excellence

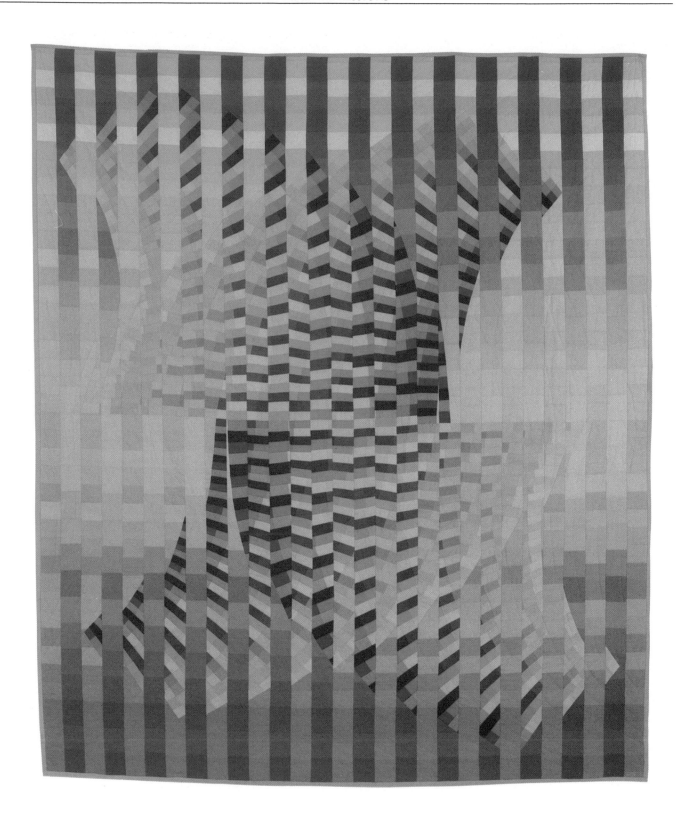

Inge Hueber
Köln, West Germany
Reflected Image
Self-dyed cotton; cotton batting. Machine pieced, hand quilted.
78″ x 94″

The source of inspiration and motivation for a new quilt begins for me with my self-dyed cotton. The unlimited variety of colors and their relationship to one another fascinate me. The handwork involved with the use of these materials provides me with joy and satisfaction. Fabric offers me the opportunity, through putting together and cutting apart, through displacing and replacing, to preserve a variety of planned and unplanned color and form connections. Going beyond this is the quilting, which provides an additional structuring of the surface through the effect of light and shadow.

Nancy Gipple
St. Paul, Minnesota
Rock Garden for Donald & Verdell
Cotton and cotton blend fabrics, cotton batt. Predominantly machine stitched. 94" x 104"

What interests me is what exists between people—the relationships. The motivation for this piece was an interest in the blending of Eastern and Western philosophies, attitudes and aesthetics. It was made especially for my parents.

Roxana Bartlett
Boulder, Colorado
Return/The Dreams That Wolf-Dog Told Me
Cotton and acetate satin, fabric paint, printing
ink. Painting, printing, piecing, appliqué,
quilting. 54″ x 54″

The landscape of my quilts is not real but
transformed by emotion into one which is
distilled and evocative, as in a memory of long
ago or a dream. The series "The Dreams That
Wolf-Dog Told Me" draws from the spirit of fairy
tales and myths in which humans and animals
can take each other's shapes and identities.

Mary Petrina Boyd
Bellevue, Washington
Change Ringing
Cotton and cotton blend fabrics, cotton/poly
batting. Patchwork, quilting. 79″ x 55″

Change ringing is a style of ringing large church
bells which has developed in England. The bells
are rung in succession following mathematical
patterns rather than musical tunes. Somehow the
flow of color in this piece suggests the waves of
tones and overtones which flow from the bells.
The serpentine shapes are even suggestive of the
bell ropes. Then the movement and title suggest
the changes that constantly happen in our lives,
which are not static but always in the midst of
process. (More on change ringing can be found
in Dorothy Sayers' novel *The Nine Tailors*).

Peggy Spaeth
Cleveland Heights, Ohio
Squares and Stars
Artist-dyed cotton, polyester batting. Machine pieced, hand quilted. 71″ x 86″

This quilt is from the collection of David Szynal.

Ruth B. McDowell
Winchester, Massachusetts
Meadow Saffron
Cottons, silks, blends. Machine pieced, hand appliquéd, machine quilted. 89″ x 67″

"Meadow Saffron *(colchicum autumnale)*" blooms in the fall after its bright green leaves have vanished—a rosy lavender cup with bright orange anthers—about six inches high. Its rare cousin *(c. autumnale album)* is a more delicate flower and a pure creamy white.

Louise Silk
Pittsburgh, Pennsylvania
City Quilts III
100 percent cotton, Cotton Classic batting.
Machine pieced and hand quilted. 95″ x 95″

My goal as a contemporary quiltmaker is to
expand the definition of a quilt, to establish new
and exciting parameters appropriate for today's
art. Since the major element in patchwork is the
block, "City Quilts III" is the third in a series
which emerges from a quilt block into a three-
dimensional sculpture. In this quilt each block is
irregular, overlapping another and taking on a
new meaning—that of a figure of some kind.

Bonnie Bucknam Holmstrand
Anchorage, Alaska
These Raindrops Are Rosie's Fault
Cottons and cotton blends, 100 percent polyester
batting. Machine pieced, hand quilted. 52″ x 52″

This piece began as an experiment with a friend's
strip-piecing method for the traditional pineapple block. The color and composition were
spontaneous and came together during construction of the blocks. To me, the completed
piece suggests reflections on the surface of a
murky pond or puddle. Raindrops—the quilting—have shattered the reflected images, leaving
behind a fractured pattern.

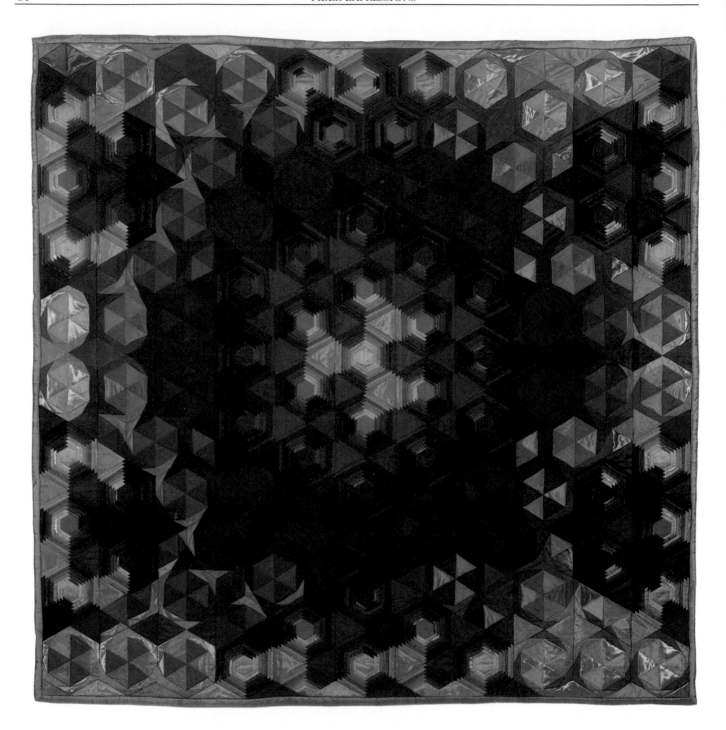

Bridget Ingram-Bartholomäus
Berlin, West Germany
Islamic Inspiration
Silk, satin, brocade, linen, cotton; acrylic filling, cotton backing.
Machine pieced; some machine quilting in the seam. 81" x 81"

This quilt was triggered by a book of Islamic geometric concepts,
at a time when I was feeling in a very red/mauve mood.

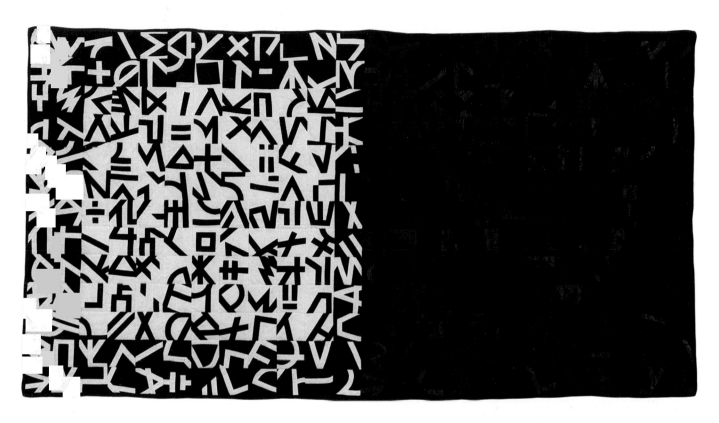

Robin Schwalb
New York, New York
Let X = X
Cottons and woolens. Machine pieced, hand quilted. 72" x 39"

In the beginning there is always color. This quilt started with the simple desire to use red and magenta together. The black and white were added to heighten the graphic quality of the design; they also suggested printing on a page. I liked the idea of the suggestion of language, rather than the actual spelling out of a message. There are whole and partial English, Greek, Hebrew and Russian letters as well as astrological, mathematical and electronic symbols. For the past two years I have been working on a series of "contained" crazy quilts, using patterns for the individual squares. "Let X = X" is a logical extension of this technique. Each pattern was used twice, so that the designs of the two halves of the quilt correspond exactly. "Let X = X" is the title of a song by performing artist Laurie Anderson.

Françoise Barnes
Colorado Springs, Colorado
Misumena Ellipsoides
Cotton, cotton blends, silk, polyester batting. Machine pieced by
Françoise Barnes and Bill Smith, hand pieced by Françoise
Barnes, hand quilted by Susan Hershberger. 88″ x 88″

MISUMENA is the name of a small yellow spider whose potent
poison paralyzes her victims; she is, however, beautiful. To
marvel at the extraordinary beauty of some insects, to be
intrigued by their mysterious world and to study them under the
microscope is certainly not new; what is new is my effort to do so
via the medium of quiltmaking. "Misumena Ellipsoides" is the
first of a series openly dedicated to ontomorphic designs where
color, as always, will keep its dominant role. I have let this spider
of now gigantic proportions invade my quilt to allow her to
display some of her beauty for everyone to see. Here's to you,
Miss UMENA!

Virginia Jacobs
Philadelphia, Pennsylvania
Krakow Kabuki Waltz
Cottons, chintz and blends; latex balloon armature. Machine pieced and quilted. 84″ diameter

"Krakow Kabuki Waltz" developed out of my interest in exploring the sculptural possibilities in quilting. Since few "art quilts" function today as bed quilts, there is no longer any strict necessity for quilting as an art form to be limited to a flat rectangular format. This three-dimensional work is named in honor of two of the visual cultures that I find most colorful and inspiring graphically.

Anyone familiar with the detailed geometric designs of Ukranian pysanky will recognize another source of inspiration. I am concerned with the musical rhythms created by the repeating and contrasting colors, shapes and patterns of the fabric pieces. These smaller rhythms function not only as a measure to give scale and energy, but also as the components in the overall composition that make up the two end star sections and the directional movement of the pastel sequence around the equator. I want the viewer to become involved spatially with my work as it evolves as the viewer moves around it. I also think I just wanted to make something that was absolutely outrageous.

Most Innovative Use of the Medium Award

Jane Burch Cochran
Burlington, Kentucky
Ceremonial Cloth: Zuni Roses
Fabric, paint, buttons, beads, sequins. Machine pieced, hand sewn and appliquéd with beads. 38″ x 45″

"Ceremonial Cloth" was inspired by a book which told of several American Indian ceremonies performed by medicine women. I could see them covering the feathers, stones or other objects used in the ceremony with such a cloth. This piece was also inspired by some old silk ribbon I bought in New York that is seen in the centers of the "Zuni Roses."

Photographed by the artist.

Susan Webb Lee
Oak Ridge, North Carolina
Mozambique
Cotton and cotton/polyester fabrics; cotton/poly batting. Machine pieced and machine quilted. 66″ x 66″

I began making quilts in 1979. My first ones were hand painted with Procion dyes and were usually hand quilted. They were painted on one width of fabric and involved little or no piecing. In my current work, I do a minimum of fabric dyeing; instead I concentrate on intricate piecing techniques, color relationships and design. I start each quilt by choosing fabrics that I feel work well together, and I almost always include black. My color selections often change during the construction of a quilt, and the design itself continually evolves. I design each quilt as I go, pinning fabrics to my work wall and adding or deleting as I progress. This gives me the option of rearranging areas, adding colors, or being a bit spontaneous. The most exhilarating part of working this way is when all the pieces start to look as though they belong to the same quilt.

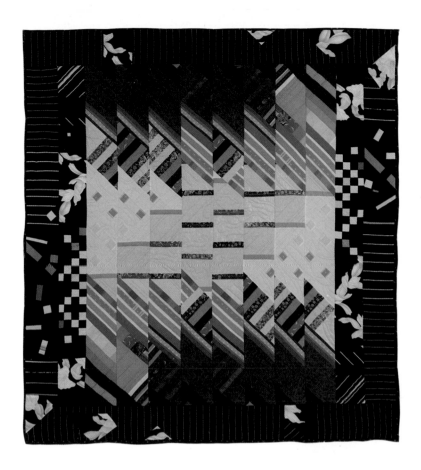

Judi Warren
Maumee, Ohio
Blossoms and Breaks
Cottons and hand-dyed viscose satins. Machine pieced, hand quilted. 50″ x 55″

"Blossoms and Breaks," the second in an on-going series of "Blossoms" quilts, is about the contrast between floral imagery and hard-edged pieced shapes, and about pattern and continuity that is established, then shifted and begun again. Linear elements of strip-pieced fabric about eight feet long were joined to form a large parallelogram which was then cut diagonally into strips and reassembled out-of-sequence to create new relationships and visual interruptions—hence the title "Blossoms and Breaks." Hand quilting echoes the white blossoms that are sprinkled around the quilt's edge.

Michele Walker
Brighton, England
Aquarius
Cotton fabric, synthetic batting, satin ribbons. Machine stitched and quilted. Geometric shapes with applied ribbons folded and stitched to the quilted surface. 29″ x 29″

I have always made "flat quilts," but this time felt that I would like to explore the effects of pleating and folding fabric. The folds were emphasized by the rippling lustre of the applied ribbons. I especially like the way the design changes according to the source of light.

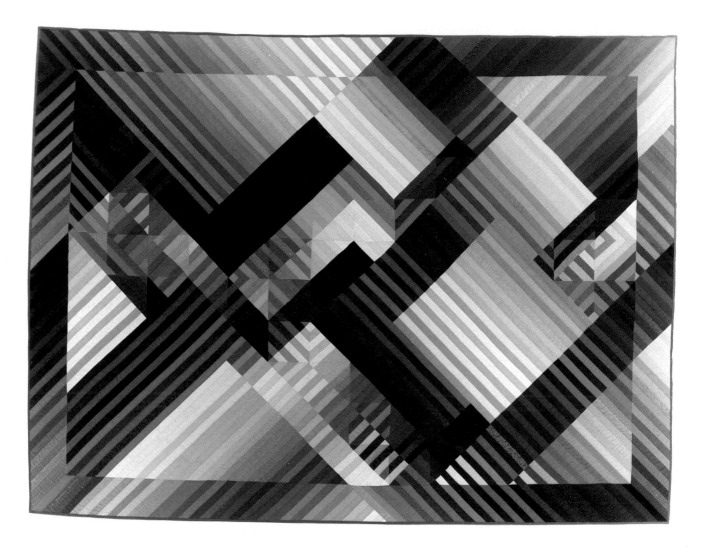

Michael James
Somerset Village, Massachusetts
Bias Cut
Cotton and silk; cotton batt. Machine pieced and machine quilted. 88″ x 67″

A primary goal in my work has been, and continues to be, the creation of visual surfaces in which the viewer can encounter unexpected color/space juxtapositions and complex movements which will appear to have changed after multiple viewings. I want the viewer to discover new elements each time the object is seen and to feel that familiarity with the work intensifies rather than diminishes each successive encounter.

Darcy Usilton
Madison, Wisconsin
Blessed Darcy Taming
Upholstery fabrics, velvets, embroidery thread,
yarns, metallic thread. Hand sewn. 69″ x 45″

I saw an antique art screen in Minneapolis
decorated with a dragon and tiger. The plaque
beside the screen told me that the tiger and
dragon are symbols of creativity in Japan. I
frequently use dragons in my work and I love
cats. At the time, I was also thinking of incorporating St. Margaret into the work (myth says she
tamed a dragon). Of course the hours spent
sewing turned my thoughts to the fact that I just
as easily could tame creativity. That explains the
title "Blessed Darcy Taming." I didn't want to be
called a saint—naked as I was in the piece of
artwork—but I did want it to be a strong
statement about an artist and creativity.

Detail

Jerri Finch-Hurley
Belfast, Maine
Wind
Pigment on cotton poplin, batting; a combination of airbrushing and hand painting. Machine quilted. 32″ x 28″

I create my own quilts, my own fabric swatches, my own landscapes. What I make are "quilt-scapes." "Wind" is the eleventh in this series; the first was done in 1984. I paint my images and then treat them as quilts.

"Wind" is on loan for Quilt National '87 courtesy of its owner, Pamela Cilkamini-Venanzi of Morris Plains, N.J.

Laurie Jacobs
Shaker Heights, Ohio
Hen Party
Color Xerox transfer to cotton and blends. Hand and machine stitched and quilted. 27″ x 23″

"Hen Party" was inspired by the visual personalities of a group of chickens as they awaited preparation for dinner in my kitchen.

Debra Turner Strother
Cadiz, Kentucky
Great Blue Herons
Cotton and polyester fabrics, polyester batting, acrylic paint.
Hand appliquéd and hand quilted. 70″ x 77″

"Great Blue Herons" is completely my own design. The quilting on the birds was planned to emulate feathers. This quilt was designed to hang on the wall, and is the first in a series of wildlife quilts.

Becky Schaefer
San Anselmo, California
Requiem
Fabric collage: antique Japanese silks, hand-dyed cottons (Ciba), color Xerox. Machine pieced, machine and hand quilted, machine embroidery. 59″ x 36″

The partition on the central piece of Japanese silk strongly reminded me of the Vietnam War Memorial in Washington, D.C. The concept of a "requiem quilt" grew out of that association: requiem for my sister, for lost childhoods, for dreams envisioned but not realized.

Ikuko Fujishiro
Chibaken, Japan
Flower in Full Bloom
Silk and silk antique Japanese kimonos. Hand pieced, hand dyed, appliquéd. 76″ x 108″

I patched 5,978 pieces of kimono silk which my mother gave me and created "Flower in Full Bloom." The frame is dyed by hand and is appliquéd. The pattern of flowers is made of antique fabric. Before I was 10 years old I was fascinated with the patchwork of a bed cover in a magazine, and have since become enslaved by making such works.

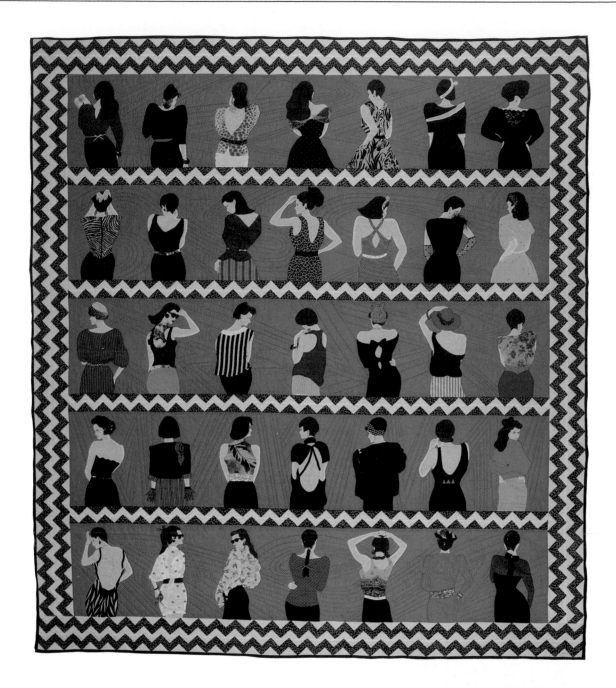

Michiko Sonobe
Tokyo, Japan
Cafe Bar
Cotton. Hand appliquéd. Quilted by Kaoru
Sonobe. 98″ x 110″

The back figure is created with patchwork and I
had a hard time collecting the materials for it and
making the many poses with variations only in
the shoulder, back and waist. I also spent much
time finding fabric for the appliqué. There are
various expressions in man's back style. I found
these styles at a fashionable café-bar. The main
theme is the creating of the mood of backs.

Detail

Judy Mathieson
Woodland Hills, California
Nautical Stars
Cotton fabrics, polyester batting. Machine and hand pieced, hand quilted. 73″ x 88″

I have been making variations of compass designs for seven years. A network of quilt friends, knowing my interest, often send me source material. One of these friends sent me a photocopy of a compass rose watercolor by an anonymous 19th century artist (possibly a sailor) that provided the inspiration for the design arrangement of "Nautical Stars." The seventeen stars were drafted using as examples map compasses and other "rose" designs I have been collecting for years. The quilt came alive for me when, in an effort to force myself out of a static pattern, I decided to use value gradations in the background. This causes the values in the central compass design to also change value as the points move around the center. Abrupt value changes in the half-dropped rows of triangles caused visible swirls and created interesting movement.

**Domini McCarthy Award
for Exceptional Craftsmanship**
Co-recipient

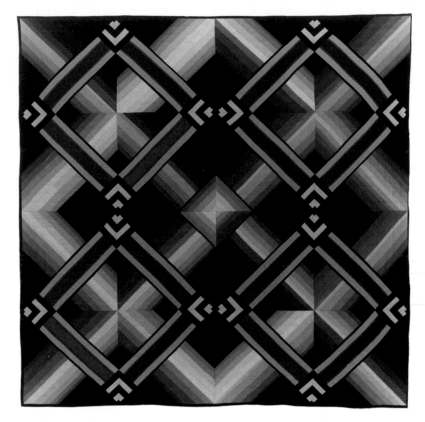

Mary Morgan
Little Rock, Arkansas
Diffraction II
100 percent cotton fabrics, some hand dyed with
Procion dyes. Machine pieced, hand quilted.
60" x 60"

Before I discovered quiltmaking I once made the
comment that I had no particular calling or
talent. How my life has changed since then! I
hope my quilts express some of the pleasure and
excitement I feel while making them.

Robin Corthell Bennett
Nikiski, Alaska
Confetti
Cotton and poly/cotton fabric, polyester batting.
Quilted with nylon thread using a machine-like
two-needle hand-quilting technique; embroi-
dered on the back with metallic gold thread.
59" x 50"

The title "Confetti" was inspired by what was left
on the floor when the front had been assembled.

Deborah J. Felix
Atlantic Highlands, New Jersey
Paper Faces/Gossip Series
Vinyl, acrylic medium, fabric, paper, rubber stamps, textile paint, canvas, stencils, batting. Machine stitched; quilted with paper fasteners. 77″ x 77″

"Paper Faces" is about the artificial worlds or words that we build our lives upon. Gossip is a wonderful source of entertainment that has kept many a person happily occupied for days, weeks or even years.

Photographed by the artist.

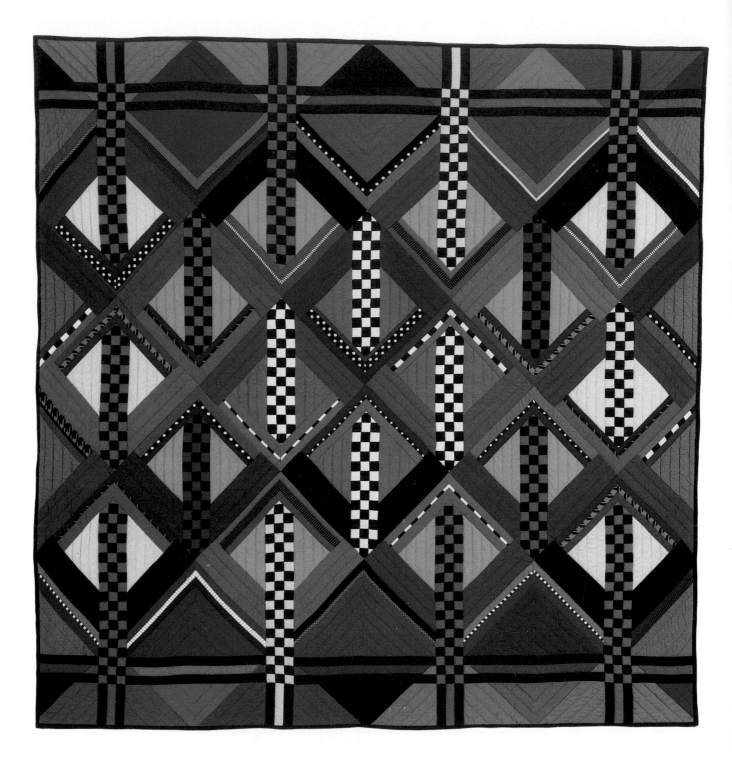

Sharon Heidingsfelder
Little Rock, Arkansas
Almost a Melody
100 percent cotton fabric with some areas silkscreened; strip piecing combined with traditional piecing. Hand quilted by Dean Simpson of Little Rock, Arkansas. 72″ x 72″

As I design my quilts, I am more interested in the division of space and color than anything else. I am not easily adept at portraying symbolism or interpreting life's experiences in fabric. My designs are done on a flat 2-D plane, and I become deeply moved when colors and shapes begin to work together.

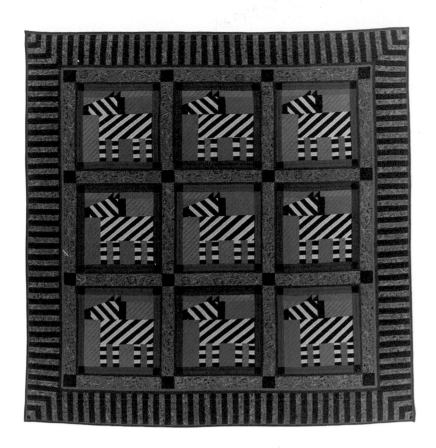

Katharine Brainard
Takoma Park, Maryland
Zebra Quilt
Machine-pieced cotton fabrics, polyester batting.
Hand quilted. 54″ x 54″

I have designed many pieced animal quilts, including cats, elephants, penguins and squirrels. In each quilt I try to stretch myself, to do something slightly different from anything that I have done before—a different technique, fabric usage or concept. In "Zebra Quilt" I used a large floral print for the first time. The floral fabric contrasts with the geometric stripes; the diagonal quilting contrasts with the cable quilting.

Lynn Last Rothstein
Athens, Ohio
Black Cheeked Man with Wrinkles
Cotton fabric, hand dyed with Procion dyes.
Machine-pieced satin fabric and ribbons machine
appliquéd. Hand quilted by Mary and Mattie
Mast. 42″ x 57″

I've been sewing for 25 years and have at various times sold clothing I designed and made. I also have for the last three years been painting abstract watercolors. My quilts are the fabric forms of my watercolors. Watercolors are my pleasure; quilts are my work.

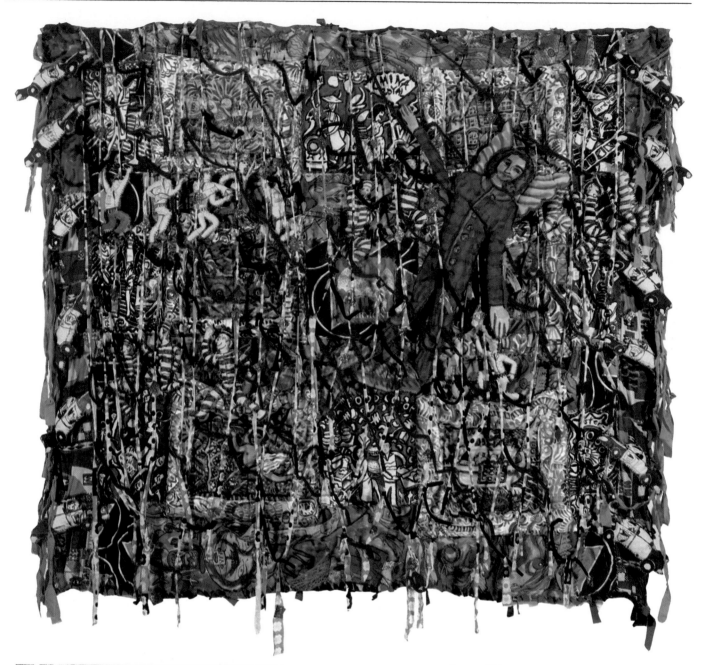

Detail

Susan Shie
Wooster, Ohio
Neighborhood with Comet Scar
Acrylic paint and fabric dye on canvas and fabric.
Stuffed and sewn painted forms, found objects,
mylar. 98″ x 88″

The blue "Vermont" ram in the center of the quilt
is the "comet scar," a sweatshirt front which
burned when a firecracker exploded on me
when I went to an observatory to view Halley's
Comet. With this symbol as my personal center, I
built my neighborhood on the quilt, which is
part of a group of six quilts called "Girl and Her
Comet," which form a diary of my life during the
1985-86 visit of the comet.

Best of Show Award

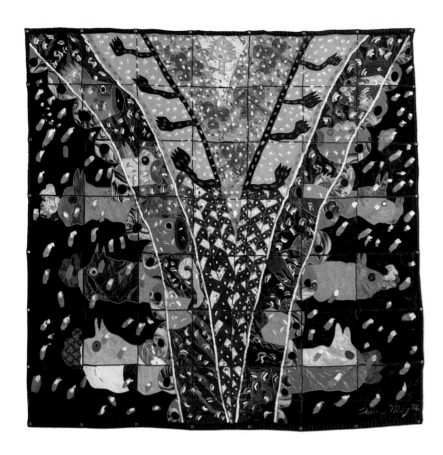

Therese May
San Jose, California
Fish and Chicks
Polyester, cotton, silk, satin, taffeta, acrylic paint.
Machine appliqué. 83" x 85"

A more apt title might be "Fish, Chicks, Tulips, Shamrocks, Braided Rug Pattern and a Christmas Tree." Fish are for the deepest feelings; chicks represent rebirth; tulips are happiness and childhood; shamrocks are for St. Patrick and the Trinity; the braided rug pattern is for home; the Christmas tree is for the Christ. I love color, pattern, fabric, paint and putting things together. Also, I love life and growing.

Laurie Jacobs
Shaker Heights, Ohio
"...but there was a faulty joint in the right rocket booster."
Color Xerox transfer to cotton and blends. Hand and machine stitched and quilted; hand painted and beaded. 37" x 37"

This piece was originally conceived as a celebration of the energy and spontaneity reflected in contemporary graffiti art and neon colors. However, the construction was abruptly interrupted by the tragedy of the Space Shuttle Challenger explosion, and the emotional impact of that event came to dominate the finished piece.

Risë Nagin
Pittsburgh, Pennsylvania
Sights in Transit
Silk, cotton, polyester, rayon, acetate. Pieced, appliquéd, embroidered, hand sewn. 61″ x 51″

"Sights in Transit" deals with perception, remembered images and peripheral sights. The guardrails that run along the edge of the highway are part of the landscape, seen and unseen as one drives. Noticed over time in snatches, they have been reassembled via memory into a pattern, a composite view of many places along the road...a landscape over time.

Courtesy Helen Drutt Gallery, Philadelphia, Pennsylvania.

Anneke Herrold
Greencastle, Indiana
Craziness Behind the Fence
Cotton. Machine pieced with self-binding strips on the back. 46″ x 57″

The quilt's background is made from many pieces of seemingly disparate fabrics. Because many of the fabrics were rejects (even "ugly"), the challenge was to assemble them all into a harmonious whole. The interwoven blue and black lattice seems to make a layer on top. It contains the "craziness," much as my garden fence contains the flowers, weeds and shrubs by my house.

Nancy Halpern
Natick, Massachusetts
Landfall
Cottons and blends; many hand-dyed and printed fabrics. Machine pieced, hand quilted. 80″ x 72″

Landfall: "first sighting of land after a voyage or flight." In my worklife as a traveling quilt teacher, I set foot in many landscapes. When there's time I get to wander a little, picking up stones, tasting berries, beginning the reciprocal process that makes us part of each other. In this quilt I come back to the landscape I love most, the one I carry around inside me, the one I keep trying to bring out into the light, to wrap and fold around me. But since it contains bits of memory I have buried, and stones I have yet to find (much less turn), it feels used and elusive all at once, and hovers in time between what is known, worn and touched, and tomorrow's foggy weather report.

Judith Larzelere
Dedham, Massachusetts
Sunrise: Jappa Flat
100 percent cotton, 50/50 poly cotton chintz, polyester batting.
Machine strip pieced, machine string quilted. 119″ x 94″

My images are carefully planned and color choices are very deliberate, but I work with a great deal of looseness as I begin to sew the quilt together. I try to remain open to solutions so that I can improve on my original ideas. Because of this flexibility, I have "discovered" unexpected visual events in each new quilt

that usually suggest the problems and directions for the next quilt. I am searching to develop structures that enable me to recreate the apparent artlessness of nature's organic forms. I am fascinated by the flicker of light on moving water, the shimmer of the Northern Lights, the drift of clouds, the patterning of pebbles washed up on a beach. I have a great appetite for color and enjoy using color to evoke a mood response in the viewer. "Sunrise: Jappa Flat" is my homage to the beauty I have experienced many times looking over water to the rising winter sun.

Invitational

Jane Blair
Conshohocken, Pennsylvania
Summer
Cotton and cotton/polyester fabrics. Hand pieced and hand quilted. 52″ x 65″

As a lover of the Impressionistic period of painting, it seemed like a good idea to try the same idea in fabric. Since all my quilts begin with a traditional block, "Summer" started with the maple leaf block. In various sizes, it has been squeezed, widened, elongated, added to and subtracted from to create a view of my favorite season.

Mary Morgan
Little Rock, Arkansas
Number 30
100 percent cotton muslin, hand dyed with Procion dyes. Machine pieced, machine quilted. 58″ x 52″

More than anything else, I enjoy working with color, especially light-to-dark gradations. Dyeing my own fabrics gives me the color gradations that would otherwise be unavailable. Like most quilt-makers, I love manipulating fabrics, and dyeing provides one more level of satisfaction. It's fun to make a bolt of muslin turn into a richly colored quilt!

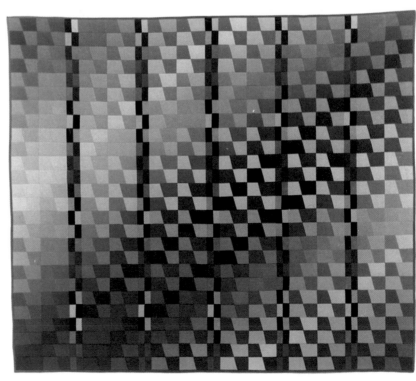

Bridget Ingram-Bartholomäus
Berlin, West Germany
Untitled
Mainly silk fabrics, with some synthetics, piping cord, cotton backing, acrylic filling. A few fabrics machine pieced to form a striped material. Hand pieced and then machine quilted, partly in sections. 57″ x 58″

Everywhere I looked I seemed to see interwoven patterns, so I decided to tackle one in patchwork. I enjoyed changing scale within a piece and like playing with color.

Nancy Whittington
Carrboro, North Carolina
Leaf Symmetry I
Hand-dyed silks, overpainted with textile paints. Hand pieced using English patchwork technique (each piece sewed over paper and then stitched together). 45″ x 45″

Repeated in myriad patterns, overlapping, ever changing in the different lights of sun and shadow, the leaf is one of the most common shapes that surrounds us. What simple symmetry —two halves connected by a central stem, striped veins pushing to the outer edge. The variation of this simple shape put to pattern is the departing point for this series of quilts.

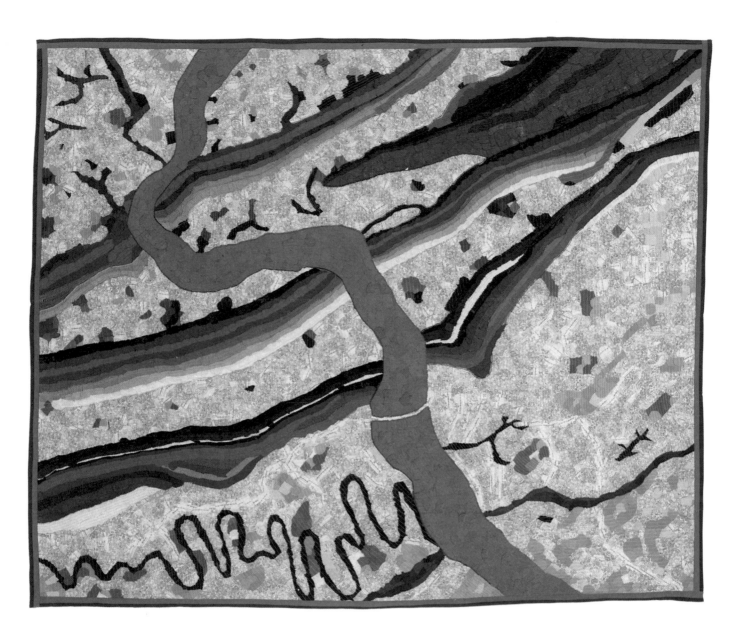

Detail

Holley Junker
Sacramento, California
Infrared River Valley
Pinked and layered cotton fabrics. Machine stitched to top; hand quilted; Xerox transferred to silk appliquéd to back. 71″ x 60″

I am fascinated by how the landscape looks from above—flying, looking down from tall buildings, mountains—colors blend, edges merge, perspective flattens. During the past several years I have been making quilts of aerial views—some real, some fantasy—employing a somewhat pointillist technique of machine stitching small pieces of fabric to a backing, then finishing by either hand quilting or tying. "Infrared River Valley" almost seems to me to be the ultimate aerial image.

Julia E. Pfaff
Richmond, Virginia
Greek Geometry in Black, Green & Blue
Cotton blends, polyester batting. Machine pieced, hand
embroidered, hand quilted. 72″ x 82″

My approach to quilting is both as an artist and as a person who
grew up with a family tradition of quilt making. I think of quilts as
having two levels. The first is a flat graphic pattern; the second, a
linear design overlaying the whole. The result should be a three-
dimensional object which retains its functional qualities as well
as the strength of design to be hung on a wall. The majority of the
embroidery on this quilt was done in Greece while I was working
on an archaeological excavation. The embroidery design was
based on Bedouin stitchery I saw while working in Egypt.

Detail

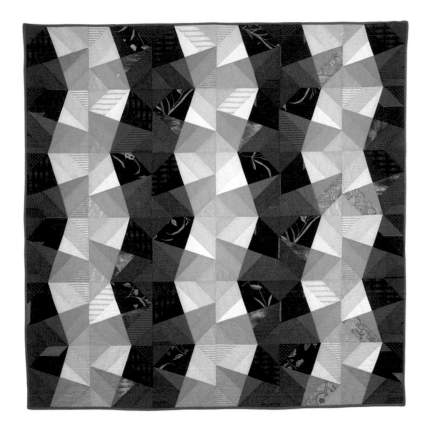

Carol Gersen
Exeter, New Hampshire
The Greens of Summer
Cottons and blends, cotton polyester batting.
Machine pieced, hand quilted, signed and dated
in quilting. 63″ x 63″

"The Greens of Summer" is the fourth quilt in a
series on seasonal themes, all using the same
block. I began with a value study and translated
the design into color by matching fabrics to the
values in the sketch. I stacked the blocks in
vertical rows to create a feeling of growing plants.

Esther Parkhurst
Los Angeles, California
The Great Divide
Cotton and blends, both solid color and print
fabrics. Strip pieced, machine quilted. 61″ x 40″

I use the properties of color, a never ending
discovery and challenge process, to develop
movement and show the quality of light and dark
in my work. I work intuitively in a trial and error
method to produce my abstract works. My
concern or interest is in dealing with movement.

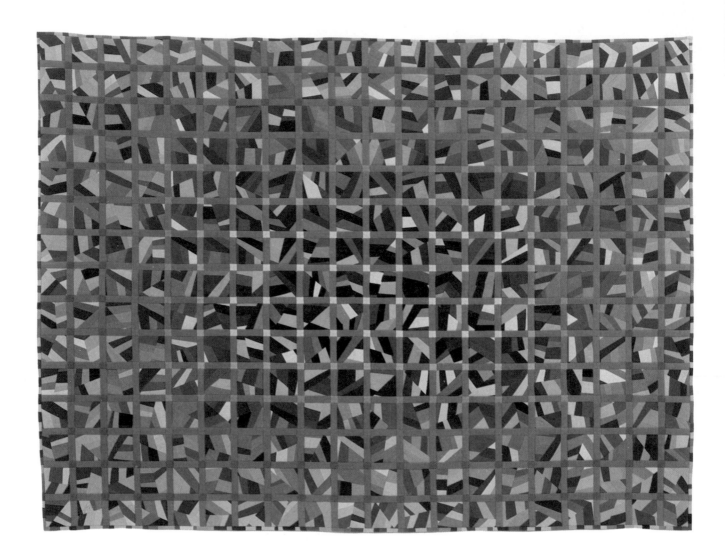

Jan Myers
Minneapolis, Minnesota
Morning Glory
Hand-dyed 100 percent cotton front and back; polyester batt.
Machine pieced and machine quilted. 69″ x 51″

This is the latest in a series of "contained crazy quilts," inspired by their traditional ancestors. I admire these quilts for their balance of order and chaos, as well as the additional spatial plane created by the lattice-work.

Invitational

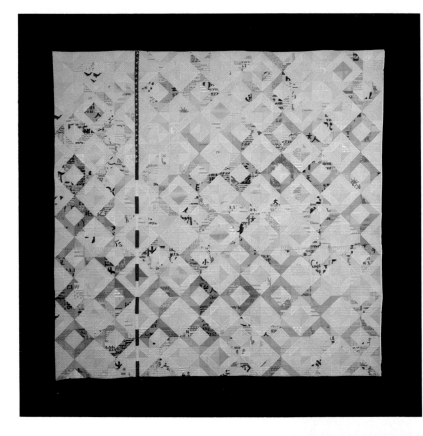

Sara Long Rhodes
Ft. Bragg, California
National Cohesion
Cotton and cotton blends. Pieced, hand stenciled and screened, hand quilted. 69″ x 68″

This quilt was conceived as a statement of hope for national and world peace, the coming together of all nations in a unified whole. "We the People...."

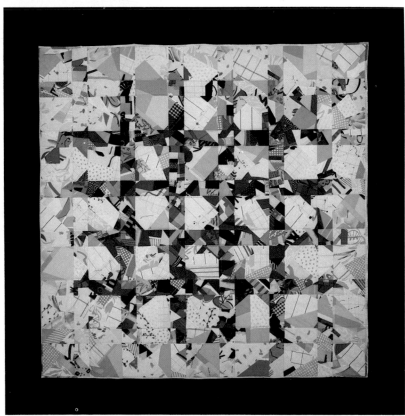

Sylvia H. Einstein
Belmont, Massachusetts
Charivari
Cottons and cotton blends. Machine pieced and machine quilted. 59″ x 59″

"Charivari" is the second of a series of quilts depicting the carnival in Basel, Switzerland. It shows the brightly costumed people milling in the streets.

Linda MacDonald
Willits, California
Chasing Red Dogs
100 percent cotton fabric, polyester batt. Machine pieced, hand appliquéd, hand quilted. 89″ x 90″

I've been running now for three years on Exley Road in Willits. There are quite a few dogs that run out, snarl and look more vicious than they actually are. But I was finally bitten on the leg: tore my pants, got a big bruise, but didn't break the skin. "Chasing Red Dogs" is about those dogs; they're quilted in red, and they move through the three-dimensional landscape diagonally up and to the right. The environment that they're in is really the quilt. I wanted to create depth in space that was fresh and stimulating without being academically dull, mechanical, or having the focus be a lesson in one and two-point perspective. The owners of the quilt, Kathleen and Robert Kirkpatrick, just happen to live on Exley Road.

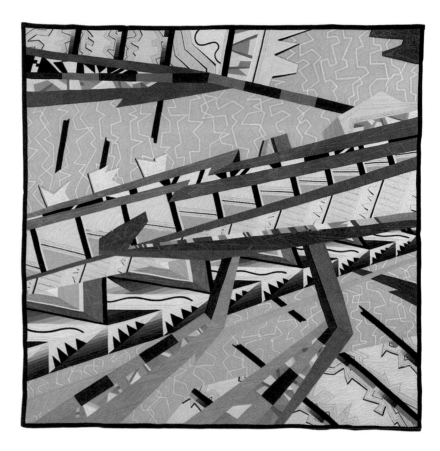

Linda MacDonald
Willits, California
Salmon Ladders
100 percent cotton fabric, polyester batt; hand painted; hand appliquéd; marbleized fabric on back done with inks. Machine pieced, hand quilted. 92″ x 92″

I wanted to use large areas of one color—salmon—in this quilt, and I wanted them to come alive because of the quilting. I knew I would need paint to help this activity. From a distance, one sees the painted lines; from closer, one sees both. The paint and the quilting accentuate and activate each other. I like the results. I also used paint here and there throughout the quilt to add a thicker, heavier linear element—one not quite large enough to become a shape. The center of the back is made of hand-marbleized fabric done with Pelikan inks.

This quilt is from the collection of Sandra Metzler and Mark Rawitches, Willits, California.

Barbara Mortenson
Melrose Park, Pennsylvania
Breaking Loose
Cottons and cotton blends. Machine pieced, hand appliquéd, hand quilted. 74″ x 65½″

Breaking loose from tight structures and rules has always been a struggle and a part of my life. I'm interested in what is released when one does break loose.

Julia R. Swan
Cambridge, Ohio
The Raggedy Men
The materials for the figures are all wool or part wool. The background is corduroy going various directions so the pile adds texture. I added embroidery to give a hint of an old crazy quilt. 53″ x 35″

I saw a black and white drawing by Steig which inspired the piece. I have so many beautiful wool scraps from clothes I make, and I like to find uses for them in quilts. The figures turned out much more sinister looking in fabric than they had in the sketch. Spacing the figures in two groups also suggests sinister dealings.

Detail

Caryl Bryer Fallert
Oswego, Illinois
High Tech Tucks V
100 percent hand-dyed cotton, wool batting.
Dyed, pieced, pleated, twisted and quilted.
47″ x 41″

This is the fifth in a series of quilts incorporating twisted constructed tucks into a pieced background. The background is composed of rectangles dyed in a 14-step gradation between black and white. One side of each tuck is also made from one of the shades in this gradation. The other side is made from a 19-shade gradation from green to blue to purple to fuschia. The tucks are constructed separately and inserted into the seams of the background. They are then twisted and sewn with curving lines of quilting to give the illusion of movement over the quilt's surface.

The sub-title "Cold Wave" refers to a week of bitterly cold weather in early November 1985 while I was working on the quilt. The undulation of the tucks reminded me of the cold winds outside.

This quilt is from a private collection.

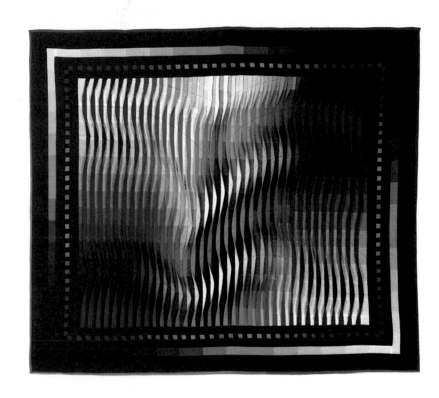

Esther Parkhurst
Los Angeles, California
Connections II
Cotton and blends, both solid color and print fabrics. Strip pieced, machine quilted. 63″ x 63″

I use the properties of color, a never ending discovery and challenge process, to develop movement and show the quality of light and dark in my work. I work intuitively in a trial and error method to produce my abstract works. My concern or interest is in dealing with movement.

Katherine Knauer
New York, New York
Air Force
Self-drawn stencils and airbrushed fabric paint on cotton, embroidery, beads. Machine pieced, hand quilted. 74½″ x 77″

Everything about "Air Force" is a triptych: the title itself is a triple play on words referring to the U.S. Air Force, the Force of Heaven, and the power of the air brush which was used in the creation of the quilt itself. This is one of an ongoing series of figurative quilts dealing with the subject of warfare.

Kumiko Sudo
San Jose, California
Revelation
Silk, cotton, rayon. Pieced, layered, appliquéd, embroidered, painted, dyed. 78″ x 90″

"Revelation" depicts a time when God leads the human family to a new world of joy and beauty.

Kathi Casey
Dallas, Texas
Night Chasms
Cottons, cotton sateens, cotton blends painted with metallic fiber paints. Machine pieced, hand quilted. 60″ x 60″

I try to create quilts which let the viewer's eye "play" with the surface—always seeing new and different things as you look at it longer. In "Night Chasms" the quilting designs in the black complete an overall surface design with the unpredictable painted metallic shapes. The border is composed of several different blacks of various sheens combined with quilting to highlight the textural beauty unique to this medium.

Pamela G. Johnson
Kansas City, Missouri
Black and White Log Cabin, © *1985*
Cotton; poly/cotton batting. Machine pieced, hand quilted. 49″ x 49″

The log cabin pattern interests me as a simple structure on which to base experiments with color and pattern. A single print of black and white equilateral triangles was cut apart and forced to take on an appearance quite different from the original fabric. The reduced palette of red, white and thirteen variations of black intensifies the level of abstraction and emphasizes my interest in non-objective forms.

Anne Woringer
Paris, France
Urubamba
Cottons and polished cottons, polyester batting. Machine pieced, hand appliquéd, hand quilted. 69″ x 67″

This work was done in a depressive moment of my life. I used very brilliant colors to react against sadness. I realized the quilt very quickly, frantically, and it gave me real happiness.

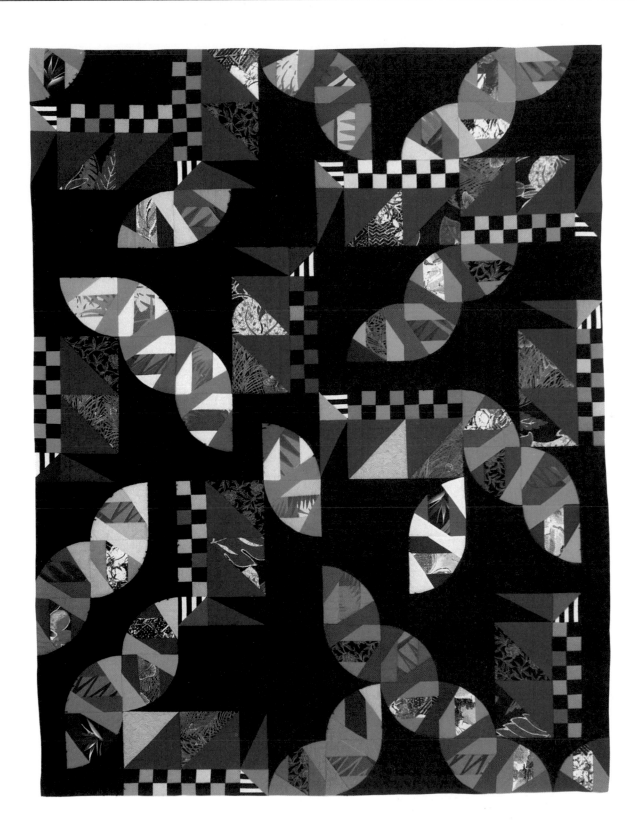

David Walker
Cincinnati, Ohio
Centersearch
Cottons and cotton blends. Machine pieced, machine and hand quilted, hand knotted. 58″ x 76″

I have found that my work is often being pulled in several directions. Many themes and expressions are struggling for my time and attention. Centering seems to be a key theme for my own personal happiness and sense of harmony. So many voices are competing for the attention of the artist. To hold at bay and to be able to set aside for a time the myriad possibilities demanding the artist's attention, it is necessary to focus in on the work at hand and to center one's concentration on the present problem. For me, my art is a constant conversation between myself and the idea being expressed in the quilt. I cannot be a good listener if my attention is being distracted by other voices.

Pauline Burbidge
Nottingham, England
Still Life Quilt I
100 percent cotton fabrics, polyester filling.
Machine pieced and appliquéd, machine quilted.
52″ x 54″

The imagery of this work has grown from a series
of paper collages of still life subjects (bowls,
draped fabric, etc.) which I produced in the early
months of 1986. It is an attempt to work a little
more freely, yet I still cling to the traditional
repeated block as my main structure for this
quilt.

W. Kim Messier
Kittery Point, Maine
NYCity
Appliqué fabric, plastic tubing, ink, pencil.
58″ x 68″

My quilts are a way of experimenting—another attempt to amaze myself.

Bonnie J. Thornton
Albuquerque, New Mexico
The Turquoise Trail
Cottons, cotton/polyester, Cotton Classic batting.
Machine pieced, hand quilted. 72″ x 72″

"Turquoise Trail" reflects the colors, patterns and emotions of the Southwest, where I have lived for two years. It is named for my favorite road from Albuquerque to Sante Fe, which I have traveled many times getting to know my new home. Surprisingly, the original inspiration came from the Navajo-like patterned fabric, which my husband spotted as we searched through a warehouse in Adams, Massachusetts, eight years ago.

Laura Lee Fritz
Inverness, California
And Crown Her Good with Brotherhood
Cotton fabrics, cotton/polyester blends. Hand embroidered and
hand appliquéd. 71″ x 71″

Freedom and Liberty: embroidered with single strands of thread,
hand appliquéd 20 stitches per inch. Every man, woman and
child is a hero, celebrated here, as are our forefathers standing
beside us (the black silhouettes). We are surrounded by
creatures of the wild quilted into the outer border.

**Domini McCarthy Award
for Exceptional Craftsmanship**
Co-recipient

Pauline Burbidge
Nottingham, England
Diagonal Zig-Zag
100 percent silk fabric-pieced top, cotton backing
fabric and cotton filling. Machine pieced and
machine quilted. 52″ x 52″

This quilt is deliberately designed with a simple,
stark, austere and pure shape—allowing the
texture of the cloth and quilting to play a
significant role in the work.

Alex Fuhr
Oxford, Ohio
Quilt
Fiber reactive dye on rayon challis and cotton
broadcloth. Rayon machine pieced onto cotton
inner piece and then hand quilted to rayon back
pieces. Hand hemmed. Hand quilted by Twila
Fuhr and the artist. 68″ x 86″

I believe that if an object is to be called a quilt it
must be something under which one would wish
to sleep. Art works that deal only with quilt
imagery should not be confused with the real
thing. Nonfunctional art-quilts might more aptly
be called collage or mixed media.

Michiko Sonobe
Tokyo, Japan
Vakansu
Cotton. Hand appliquéd. Quilted by Kaoru Sonobe. 81″ x 85″

I simply wanted to make original work. I tried to express the fun of a vacation with appliqué and patchwork; to create a feeling of light, air, motion and expression; and to give depth to the figures. I imagine the softness of the fabric as the gentleness of women.

Risë Nagin
Pittsburgh, Pennsylvania
Road Goliaths
Acrylic paint, silk, polyester, cotton, acetate. Stained fabrics, layered, pieced, appliquéd, embroidered, hand sewn. 71″ x 56″

The Biblical figure Goliath was the giant Champion of Philistia. A warrior of great might, he intimidated the armies of Saul. "Road Goliaths" is a portrait of trucks which are, in a sense, the macho champions of commerce, dominating their highway territories and intimidating smaller vehicles on the road.

Courtesy Helen Drutt Gallery, Philadelphia, Pennsylvania.

Elizabeth S. Gurrier
Hampton, New Hampshire
Fragments
Cotton; polyester batting. Hand painted with fiber pigments, machine and hand quilted. 41″ x 39″

"Fragments" was a study in color, texture and fragmented pattern. Having worked in white for 12 years, I find every colored quilt is a revelation and education.

Linda Levin
Wayland, Massachusetts
What You Remember Is Saved
Cottons; Procion dyes. Hand and machine
pieced. 57″ x 42″

In my work, I try to capture a scene remembered
or a particular moment in time, as well as the
feelings they called forth. For the past two years,
I've worked exclusively with fabrics I've dyed
myself with Procion dyes very freely applied,
because they make possible the spontaneous
look I want.

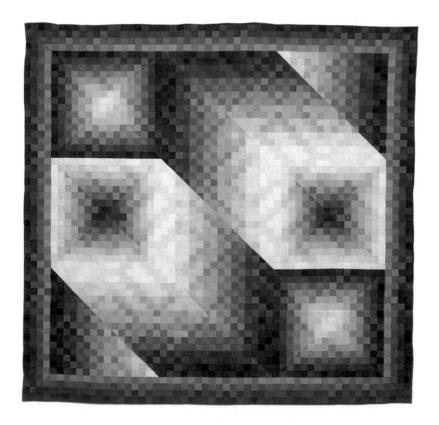

Debra Millard
Englewood, Colorado
Plains Geometry
Hand-dyed cottons (Procion fiber-reactive dyes).
Machine pieced, hand quilted, computer patterns.
80″ x 77″

This work is characterized by three elements.
The first is hand-dyed fabrics which create subtle
gradations of color. Secondly, I use a computer to
create rotations, mirror images and shifted
reproductions of a single "design module."
Lastly, there is a three-dimensional illusion
created by the juxtaposition of different color
values. I see my quilts as puzzles that need to be
solved. This is an extension of my fascination
with jigsaw puzzles and kaleidoscopes.

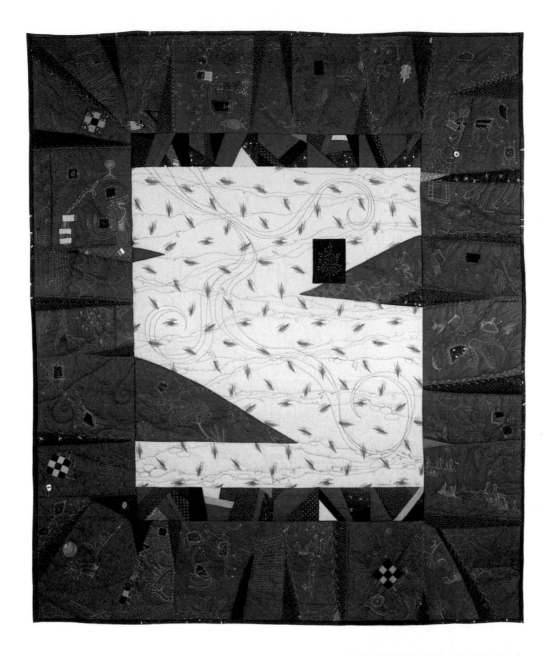

Damaris Jackson
Minneapolis, Minnesota
Lines from the Park
Calico and upholstery cottons, polyester batting,
buttons and brooches. "Drawing" with a long-
arm darning machine, piecing, appliqué. Trees
are discharge dyed and cut away. Border has two
layers of batting. 83″ x 98″

The front of this quilt is a variation on crazy
quilting; the back a variation on the Amish bars
design. The stitching on the crazy quilt patches
began as experiments in doodling and evolved
into scenes suggested by the park near my house.
The park theme unifies my interest in portraying
trees, people and animals, and it connects me
with my neighborhood. The principal challenge
was in making the center fabric and design work
without overpowering the border. I did not want
a "picture" in a frame.

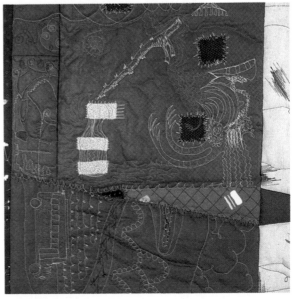

Detail

Marianne McCann
San Francisco, California
Heffer and Peffer
Cottons; cotton batting. Batiked, pieced, appliquéd, hand quilted. 35" x 40"

As children, my brother and I listened to fairy tales my grandmother invented for us using two dogs as metaphors for ourselves. The dogs had an old witch as a traveling companion and embarked on many marvelous journeys, oftentimes walking through fields and prairies on their way to adventure. "Heffer and Peffer" is based on the stories my grandmother told.

Elaine Plogman
Cincinnati, Ohio
Winter Storm Warning
Cottons and cotton blends, polyester batting. Machine pieced, hand quilted. 47" x 61"

One of my goals in designing a quilt is to establish several rhythmic lines to lead the eye of the viewer from top to bottom, right to left, corner to corner, and foreground to background. This is my way of infusing a feeling of motion into pieced quilt design, a medium inclined toward rigidity.

Yvonne Porcella
Modesto, California
Taking the Greyhound to Bakersfield
Cotton fabrics, Cotton Classic batting, hand-painted border fabrics, buttons and ornaments. Machine piecing, hand appliqué, hand quilting, photo transfer. 71″ x 75″

This quilt was done as an expression of Americana. The theme used was stars and faces. On the front surface are small images of two presidents, the Statue of Liberty and flag bunting. The fabric of Pope John Paul II was printed in Cameroon and sent to me by quilter Nancy Halpern. I couldn't wait to use it! I had one full panel and a fragment so decided to make a two-sided quilt utilizing every bit of fabric. The Pope is coming to California in 1987, so the California flag is included, as is the papal flag and that of Cameroon. The painted fabric borders create a frame for the central patchwork, with the front side border decorated with embellishments. The title is as unique as the quilt. Where else to see Americana, faces, stars and maybe the Pope, but on the Greyhound to Bakersfield?

Donna M. Stader
Indianapolis, Indiana
Antiqua
Appliqué, piping, tucking. Machine pieced and
hand quilted. 93″ x 45″

At present I am attempting to create work that
reflects the variations on a theme that can be
found in classical music. I hope that the theme is
seen with pauses, repetitions and changes of
color and tone as you view the piece.

Ellen Oppenheimer
Oakland, California
Broken Arm Quilt
Machine pieced and machine quilted. 72″ x 72″

I started this quilt without a clear image of how
the finished piece would look. I wanted to put
fabric together boldly and simply without being
too precious about craft. As I progressed, each
decision initiated the next direction. By the time
I was finished I was tremendously challenged by
craft—just the antithesis of my original concept. I
intend for this to be used on a bed—theoretically
a restful place. Paradoxically, there is constant
turmoil and movement in this quilt—no place to
rest and no room to hide. During the time I was
working on this quilt I broke a bone in my left
wrist. Most of the piecing was done with my arm
in a cast. Hence the name.

Deborah J. Felix
Atlantic Highlands, New Jersey
Bob in the Bathtub
Vinyl, canvas, commercial fabrics, hand-painted and woodblock-printed fabric, rubber stamps, plastic leaves, batting. Appliqué, reverse appliqué, quilted by Lynn Kough. 101″ x 82″

Being caught off guard while in the bathtub is a situation that's both awkward and vulnerable. So what can one do but smile at the camera?

Joyce Schlotzhauer
Painted Post, New York
Attic Layaways
Cottons, including some from the early 1900s and 1930s. Machine pieced. Hand embroidered, appliquéd and quilted. 70″ x 72″

Just past the stairs, American building blocks are stored on the attic floor as a legacy for future generations. Stacked under Liberty's crown, the teaching toys star people of all colors who shaped our nation and portray democratic values, daily concerns and pursuits. I see the inquisitive child in the toy blocks, the mother-teacher in the graphic appliqué and the protective father in the architectural shelter.

Invitational

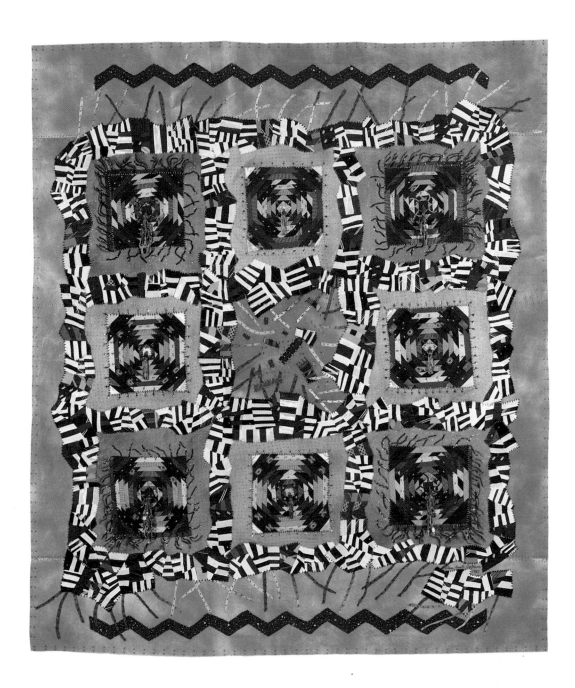

Jane Burch Cochran
Burlington, Kentucky
Crazy Quilt for a Half-Breed
Fabric (including my father's neckties), beads. Machine pieced, hand appliquéd with beads. 79″ x 93″

The pineapple quilt squares were made from my father's neckties in 1980. I pulled them out of my trunk in 1985 and combined them with the black and white piecework and other materials. While spending much of that winter beading and piecing, I fantasized myself a "half-Victorian, half-American Indian 'crazy lady.' "

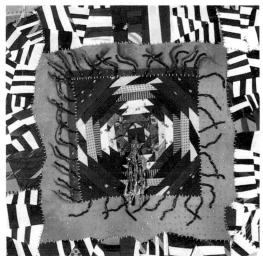

Detail

Petra Soesemann
Chicago, Illinois
Ideas for Topiary: Carnivorous Garden
Natural and synthetic fabrics, polyester batt. Machine pieced and hand appliquéd. 78″ x 78″

As a sculptor, I have become more and more interested in environment, landscape and gardens. We should have a sacred relationship to the earth, not a pragmatic one. This quilt began with the spinning shapes that form the inner and outer borders: a sense of tumbleweed, thorns, spikes...dynamic motion. Nature persists in whatever form we allow; when the environment responds to our recklessness *we* are the eventual victims.

This quilt is from the collection of Sonja Rae.

Margaret J. Miller
San Marcos, California
Rolling Thunder
Cotton and cotton/polyester fabrics; polyester batting; cotton quilting thread. Machine pieced and hand quilted. 48″ x 52″

The great joy in quiltmaking for me is in the putting together of the surface design—seeing what dimensional and color effects evolve as the quilt develops. My current interest is in the color movement across the surface of the quilt, enhanced by subtle changes in block design. This quilt is number nine in a series which is based on a very simple strip-pieced block. The quilt evolved as I was listening to Edna Ferber's book *Ice Palace*.

Liz Alpert Fay
Sandy Hook, Connecticut
...A Letter from Arthur
Hand-dyed cotton, hand-painted raw silk, solid and patterned commercial fabrics, cotton batting. Hand stitched, appliqué and reverse appliqué, machine quilted. 51″ x 44½″

This quilt was inspired by a secret code that my grandfather wrote to me as a child. After his death I came upon one of these secret letters and decided to write something about him in the code. The technique of reverse appliqué and the random use of bright colors were chosen to recall the type of drawings that children do in which black crayon is scratched away to reveal the colors beneath.

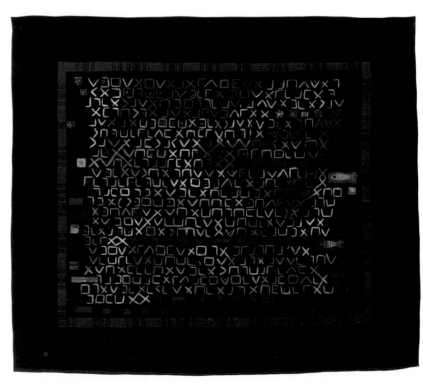

Connie Oliver
Pittsburgh, Pennsylvania
Revenge of the Scrolls
Cotton and cotton blends. Hand appliquéd, hand quilted, painted. 47″ x 56″

This piece resulted from some time a friend and I spent looking at the book of Zechariah in the Old Testament (especially Chapter 5) and dreaming of treating the awesome theme of the End Times as current suspense/horror films would—hence a slightly cockeyed, humorous look at a frightening theme.

Leslie C. Carabas
Berkeley, California
Chairs
Cottons and blends. Machine pieced and quilted. 57″ x 52″

This quilt fragments the images in an attempt to surprise the eye. I love the juxtaposition and random combination of pieces and parts of a familiar object. The long-term effect is to give the viewer new shapes to enjoy after the initial impact of the piece is over.

Katie Pasquini
Eureka, California
Kiro-Shiro
Cottons, blends and lamé. Hand screened, machine pieced, reverse appliqué, hand quilted. 87″ x 88″

This quilt is a direct result of my teaching tour to Japan. Some of the bright colored fabrics were purchased there. The Japanese flag is a circle in a square.

Invitational

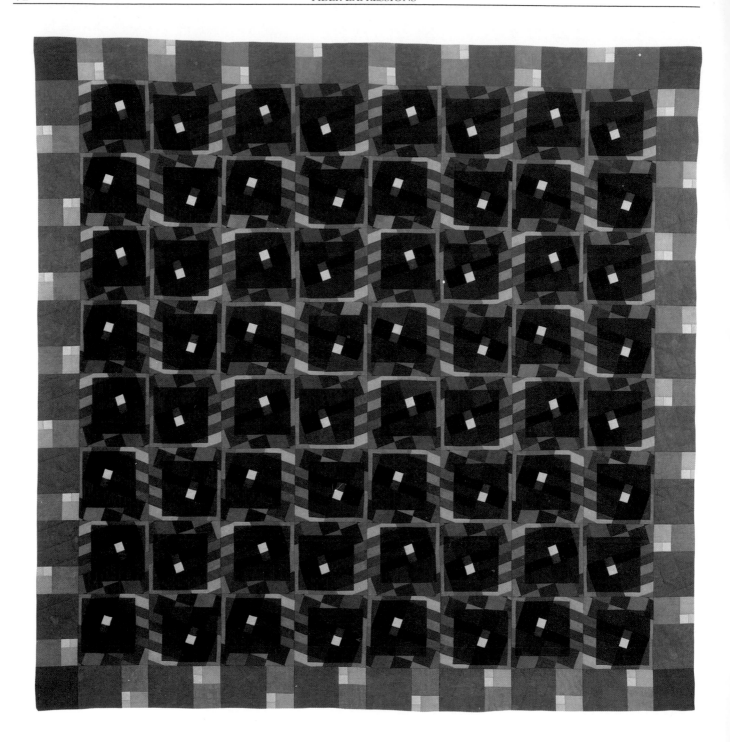

Chris Wolf Edmonds
Lawrence, Kansas
Symmetry P2GG
Hand-dyed cotton. Machine pieced, hand and machine quilted.
72" x 72"

In "Symmetry P2GG" I have returned to the traditional quilt form of block repeat but have designed an asymmetrical block which is repeated in a non-traditional symmetry. Additionally, within the block design, hand-dyed values have been arranged to create a transparency illusion.

Invitational

COMMENTS FROM
THE DAIRY BARN'S EXECUTIVE DIRECTOR

For the fifth time since 1979, the Dairy Barn Southeastern Ohio Cultural Arts Center has had the great pleasure and tremendous task of producing *Quilt National.*

It actually takes a little more than two years to produce each exhibition, which means that as we are working on the 1987 exhibit we are wrapping up the 1985 show and planning for 1989!

The 89 pieces that make up *Quilt National '87* were selected from 915 works submitted by 430 artists in 44 states and 10 countries. A stronger international representation is present this year, with 10 percent of the pieces coming from nations outside the United States.

The show itself will travel overseas, touring a number of Japanese cities in early 1988. Prior to that, *Quilt National* will be featured at the new American Craft Museum in New York City and the Textile Museum in Washington, D.C. The tour, which will include approximately 50 of the works, will continue traveling throughout the United States until 1990.

Producing an international show takes a good deal of hard work, time and financial support. In addition to the work put into the quilts by the artists, there is the effort of selecting the jury, producing publications and publicity, organizing workshops, sending mailings, photographing for the catalog, booking the tour, installing the exhibit— not to mention the less than happy task of notifying artists whose works are not selected for the show.

The Dairy Barn would like to acknowledge Hilary Fletcher, Fairfield Processing Corporation, Opportunities for the Arts and Nancy Roe for their continuous support and hard work for *Quilt National* over the past five shows.

Putting together a major exhibit is similar to preparing a Thanksgiving feast requiring meticulous planning, hours of preparation and carefully selected ingredients. When it all comes together smoothly, it appears to have been no major effort at all!

Quilt National is a "feast" that has taken two years to prepare. It is our hope that viewers will savor every minute of it!

Pamela S. Parker
Executive Director
The Dairy Barn
Southeastern Ohio
Cultural Arts Center

The Dairy Barn Southeastern Ohio Cultural Arts Center, Athens, Ohio.

Quilt National '83 Installation.

ABOUT THE DAIRY BARN

The Dairy Barn Southeastern Ohio Cultural Arts Center is recognized internationally for the high quality and unique programming that has been created by its talented staff and dedicated group of volunteers.

Quilt National joins other events such as American Contemporary Works In Wood, Basketweave and the National Jigsaw Puzzle Championships and Design Exhibition to round out a diversified schedule at the Dairy Barn. Fine Arts exhibitions and festivals also add to the many uses for the 73-year old structure.

Listed on the National Register of Historic Places, the Dairy Barn is an architectural delight affording more than 7000 square feet of exhibition space. The gently rolling Appalachian foothills provide an exquisite setting for this very special facility.

Through its five Quilt National exhibitions and their accompanying lectures, workshops and publications, the Dairy Barn has played a major role in showcasing and promoting contemporary quilting as a lively and challenging art form.

QUILT NATIONAL '87 Touring Exhibition

A collection of approximately 55 pieces from Quilt National '87 will be on display at selected galleries and institutions throughout the United States and in Japan. The tour will begin in August, 1987 and continue through December, 1989. Included on the itinerary are the following:

> The Textile Museum
> 2320 S. Street, NW
> Washington, DC 20008
> August 6, 1987 - September 27, 1987

> The American Craft Museum
> 40 West 53rd Street
> New York, NY 10019
> October 30, 1987 - January 10, 1988

> Selected sites in Japan, including Daimaru
> Department Store
> Tokyo
> February, 1988 - June, 1988

> Sharadin Art Gallery
> Kutztown University
> Kutztown, PA 19530
> October 1, 1988 - October 31, 1988

> The Delaware Art Museum
> 2301 Kentmere Parkway
> Wilmington, DE 19806
> November 18, 1988 - January 8, 1989

The QUILT NATIONAL '87 Touring Exhibition is produced by The Dairy Barn Southeastern Ohio Cultural Arts Center in Athens, Ohio, and is being circulated under the auspices of Opportunities for the Arts, Columbus, Ohio.

Quilt National '83 Installation.

Quilt National '83 Installation.

Quilt National '85 Installation.

INDEX